ALMUT BOCKEMÜHL was born in 1933 in Idar-Oberstein, Germany. She studied German literature and biology and, as the mother of four children, made an intensive study of fairy tales and folk tales. She is a freelance writer, lecturer and course leader, and lives in Dornach, Switzerland. She is the author of *A Woman's Path*.

# THE TWILIGHT YEARS
## *Thoughts on Old Age, Death and Dying*

Almut Bockemühl

Temple Lodge Publishing Ltd.
Hillside House, The Square
Forest Row, RH18 5ES

www.templelodge.com

First published in English by Temple Lodge Publishing, 2016

Originally published in German under the title *Zeit des Sterbens* by Verlag Freies Geistesleben, Stuttgart, 1991

Translated by Pauline Wehrle



A CIP catalogue record for this book is available from the British Library

ISBN 978 1 906999 87 2

Cover by Morgan Creative featuring image © Iko
Typeset by DP Photosetting, Neath, West Glamorgan
Printed and bound by 4Edge Ltd., Essex

# Contents

# 1. Departing

It had now come to the point where I had to say goodbye to my mother. It was a long drawn-out goodbye, a difficult death. It has taken more than four years of intensive care, which have been psychologically very hard. The daily bodily tasks create a different and closer connection than the most intimate of conversations. There was also a great deal of these in the earlier years, but then they stopped. My mother, who was previously a good friend to me (her daughter), slowly loosened from her bodily sheaths and became more and more helpless. This separation, stage by stage, was painful for both of us.

Life brings many kinds of changes. As a child, who had enjoyed her mother's loving care, I have myself now become a mother. And my own mother has become my child who needs care.

The first thing that happened was that failing eyesight hindered her orientation in space. Then her limbs became weaker and, in the course of the following years, incapable of moving any more. Her feet couldn't walk and her hands couldn't guide a spoon to her mouth. Speaking, too, became more and more difficult, and eventually stopped altogether.

As her daughter I often sat and looked at my mother's features that were becoming so delicate and spiritualized. She became more and more like the pictures of her early childhood. It was obvious that the dying process only applied to the body. Her soul had already gone up to another plane of existence, although it was still attached to the body. It was obvious what agony she was going through, struggling with it. She was sometimes overcome by it, and her face became distorted with pain. Her skin grew pale and her hands got cold, and she was not conscious. Then her features tightened again, becoming rosy and relaxed, even cheerful, but then her words became confused. What was going on and making her suffer? During the following months and years I saw her bodily prison becoming denser and denser. Her body contracted, and became rigid and cramped. It is through bodily movement that a person radiates out into the world. If this is denied us the only way to go is inwards.

Then came the time when the tension in her limbs suddenly loosened up. They became soft and mobile, but moved as though only from outside, without there being the possibility of her taking hold of them from inside. This condition shocked me more than the previous one, but it only lasted for a few days. Her body was now merely like a doll. Something had escaped from it, and she did not want food any more.

Then came the day when all there was to see was a lifeless husk. Her expression was like that of a young girl, astonished and expectant. The following day a deep seriousness overcame her. Where is she now, the soul I loved? How can I reach her? One would like to take a few further steps with someone one has accompanied to the threshold. One is left with nothing but questions.

Later on I had the feeling that I ought to continue giving the same quiet attention that I had been practising before, with regard to the face of the departed one; in fact this now seemed to be the most important thing I could do. The hectic everyday jobs are agonizing. These pushed their way in like a wall between the living and the dead.

The departure was like an escape, like a sigh of relief on arriving in the natural solitude of Greece. Yet one still goes around under the shattering effect of everyday experience, until the night arrives when everything becomes absolutely still outside and inside.

By day, sitting on a rock beside the sea, I looked over the water, listening and reflecting. Can this picture of these flowing expanses still speak to us as they did to the ancient Greeks, who saw in them the 'Ocean of Ether' to which our souls move on after death, becoming released from imprisonment in the physical body, spreading out more and more, not yet having accustomed themselves to the expanses and the amount of light? A gull flies close to the surface of the water, nearly disappearing, and breathlessly we think we can understand how the spirit touches the earthly world and how an earthly being can dissolve in the expanses of the circumference and yet remain itself.

We however, who sit on the rock, are onlookers.

# 2. Metamorphoses

As I walk through the long grass a white butterfly flutters up, is tossed about in the wind, and disappears behind the nearest clump of bushes.

Human beings have found many images for the process of dying. One of the most beautiful of these is that of the butterfly, which discards its chrysalis, the earthly body that is no longer usable, and as a brightly coloured winged creature rises up towards the sun. Just as far from us as it is to wish that the butterfly would return to the chrysalis, it should be just as far from us to wish that the old or sick person, who has crossed the threshold, should come back into the body. 'I need a new body, for my old one is worn out,' said an old woman.

At the moment of death everything becomes new. But as for the people who are left behind, they remain helplessly beside the deserted sheath, and can only picture to themselves the upward flight of the soul.

After death the human being resembles a butterfly. But doesn't it, before this, in its attachment to the earth resemble a creeping caterpillar that is constantly occupying itself with gathering earthly matter and filling itself with it? We must not look down with contempt on the caterpillar for it is the butterfly's child. It merely changes its form, and its transition through the chrysalis stage belongs to its being.

But the one form does not go directly over into the other. Mysterious in-between forms insert themselves, in which, outwardly unseen, its whole life is concentrated within: the egg and the chrysalis. They are both totally helpless and immobile, and yet the most important transformation processes are going on inside. May we also expect to find parallel conditions in human beings? Might this possibly be in earliest infancy and the greatest old age? In this transitory time, too, a tremendous lot is happening in conditions where a great deal of help and assistance has to be given.

The caterpillar is transformed into a chrysalis by shedding its skin for the last time, after having done so several times before. This transition can happen very dramatically. The creature rears up and flings itself around trying desperately to rid itself of its last skin. The condition following this one is somewhat different in the various types. Some chrysalises remain beneath the earth, some of them roll themselves up, and some of them hang themselves by a single thread with their stomach facing forward, a gesture of defencelessness and exposure. It is like being turned inside out. The outside skin now forms a rigid capsule, whilst the inside becomes chaotic, and the new body is being built out of the chaos.

Aren't all these various conditions images of experiences that can occur to people in old age?

Doesn't an old person often suffer from being enclosed in a sheath that is getting more and more rigid? They have to wrap themselves up in their memories because sight and hearing don't permit them to relate to the world any more. They have to put themselves helplessly into the friendly or loveless hands of a carer. Meanwhile they have to experience a reorganization of all their inner forces. Death then brings them the great turning inside out. The body is discarded when it has become so brittle that a person can no longer cope with it.

Actually the process of dying extends over the whole second half of life. In the middle of life the person's soul and spirit have become attached most firmly of all to their physical bodily nature. Their spiritual nature has taken on physical form, has transformed itself into body. At this time of life a person is most of all 'an image of himself'. The first half of life consists of working one's way towards this stage, fusing more and more closely together with the bodily sheath. This is the natural path of development a human being unconsciously aims for. A healthy young body naturally develops a love of earthly existence. Human beings want to join together with the physical and search for their earthly destiny.

The route the second half of life takes, on the other hand, to release oneself again from the body, is hard work—like the ridding itself of its old skin is to the chrysalis. The close attachment of the soul to the body is loosened again. The physical-bodily nature becomes spiritualized, transformed into spirit-soul nature. This does not happen of itself, but is difficult, and requires effort. People become increasingly distanced from their own body, and it is more and more a matter of dragging one's body around.

We mostly see our task as being above all a matter of making a strong connection with earthly life. We are far too little aware of the work connected with releasing ourselves from it again. But when we make an effort to grow old in the right way, which means transforming what is earthly into what is spiritual, we are working at the transubstantiation of the earth.

In doing this it is unavoidable that the physical is being reduced and destroyed. All conscious spiritual life destroys physical substance; it is a partial death. Without this dying process going on, no spiritual achievements are possible. Socrates was actually aware of this, and therefore his own death was an exemplary model to his pupils of the final consequences of his own philosophy: 'Those who deal with philosophy in the right way do not need to strive for anything further than to die and be dead. So if this were true, then it would really be surprising if throughout their whole lives they had been striving to attain this, but when it actually reached the point, they were unwilling to have what they had been aiming and working towards for so long.'

The death of Socrates, as Plato describes, was so dignified, because here was a human being who, in full consciousness of his immortal soul, laid aside his body as a sheath he no longer needed, whilst his soul—butterfly-like—freed itself from being bound to the earth.

# 3. Star Money

A woman who was still young, but who was nevertheless so ill that she was approaching death, said one day: 'I now understand the story of the star pennies.' 'What does that tell us?' I asked. 'We have to give up everything.' One can hardly describe the coming of death more concisely or literally. Everything, to the last ounce, is demanded of us. It is not enough to give away a hat that you hardly needed any more anyway. One thing after another, right to the last piece of protective covering, has to go. The German word for corpse is a combination of the Germanic word *lika* = body, and *hama* = clothing. A shroud actually means a 'bodily sheath', and certainly was not, as the etymological dictionary describes, 'a poetic expression' but the correct description of what the last sheath of the human being actually is. This shroud is the last thing a human being has to leave behind on the path of death.

If we don't give it up willingly then it is taken away from us. The ancient Greeks spoke about the god of death, Thanatos, who pounces on human beings like a vulture, and drags them away from the earth that they did love after all.

In the Middle Ages the idea of death was cultivated in order to convert people to a more virtuous life. Death was presented in the image of a reaper. 'It is a reaper who is called death...' Human beings are perishable, like grass and flowers that fall to the scythe. There is the disturbing picture in the Apocalypse of the 'Rider on the pale Horse'. They also saw death as a huntsman who slays his victims with a bow and arrow, or as a minstrel who leads them astray with his playing. It is only a short step from here to the dances of death of the Middle Ages, a motif that was often presented after the thirteenth and fourteenth centuries, e.g. in the painting of the walls of the cemetery in the Church of the Preachers in Basel, of which only fragments remain today of course. These were meant, above all, to bring to consciousness that death makes us all equal, emperors and beggars, pope and woodsman, a noble lady and a common maid. To speak generally: everything earthly is transient.

Baroque poetry, too, present at the time of the Thirty Years War, gets its dark undertones from this:

> What do we human beings consist of! A dwelling
>   for the bitterest pain?
> An accumulation of bad luck, a will-o'-the-wisp
>   of our time,
> The scene for sharp pain and adversity,
> Thawed snow and burnt out candles.

> Life turns its back on this like on garrulous talk
>   and jokes.
> Those who have laid aside before us the weak
>   clothing of the body

And a long time ago have had all their mortality
written into the Book of the Dead,

Have ceased to exist in our minds and hearts.

So says Andreas Gryphius. And yet the idea goes back
a long way that death approaches human beings as
the great releaser who frees us from the triviality and
adversity of existence.

It frees us not only from bodily pain but from all
physical dependence. This was already being experienced 5000 years ago, as an ancient Egyptian hymn
tells us:

To whom shall I speak in this hour?
Our hearts are impudent.
Everyone wants what his neighbour has.
To whom shall I speak in this hour?
If you are soft you will go under;
the impudent ones spread themselves out over
   planet earth.
To whom shall I speak in this hour?
There are no just people, the world is full of
   evildoers beyond count.
Death now awaits me,
and behold, I am recovering,
just as if I were recovering from a severe illness.

Those who have stood before death recover. They
become free of ambition, greed, lust for power, vanity
and egoism, from all the forces that chain us to the
earth. In death lies the secret of human freedom. The

Yugoslavian Mihailo Mihailov, in an essay he smuggled out of prison, gives his own description of this. He describes in it how many people in captivity — that is, just when they are in a condition of total outer lack of freedom — arrive at a radical experience of inner freedom. Only someone who has totally renounced everything can become completely free; that is, freedom begins at the moment there is nothing more to lose. When one has accepted the last disappointment, and suffered the last loss, there arises within one a mysterious force one has been totally unaware of before.

Mihailov calls this 'the mystic experience of the lack of freedom'. Perhaps this goes in the same direction Rudolf Steiner was pointing to when he said about certain soul experiences that one can have in old age, that if dependency on the body were not so great these experiences could lead into tremendous depths simply through the fact that one is becoming older in full inner wakefulness. But this source opens up only when one is prepared 'to give up everything'.

In fairy-tale language we can call this 'the star money experience': 'And as the child stood there with nothing left, then the stars suddenly fell from heaven, and changed into golden pennies. And if it had just given away its little vest it now had a new one made of the finest linen.'

This is an external picture for an inner experience. But are we not here altogether in the sphere where inside and outside have ended and come together? Is it then surprising that Mihailov speaks of a mystic force 'that at one and the same time is active both in the depths of the human soul and also in the outer world', so that one not only perceives something in oneself but at the same time something comes to meet one from outside that helps one and leads one forward? This must have an even more shattering effect when one is imprisoned. But even if death occurs in more everyday circumstances one can notice, if one is somewhat observant, how these things suddenly grow beyond themselves and begin, without our agency, to arrange themselves in a significant way so that this moment, the weather situation, these very people, belong to this absolutely individual death, and form a significant group around the dying one.

It is generally the case that the spiritual beings to whom the guidance of human beings is entrusted acquire more and more scope for themselves the more that human beings are capable of giving up their own self will.

Many old people feel, quite instinctively, that their main task is now to let go, to let go of wishing, of being egoistic, ambitious, even to getting rid of their possessions. And the more they succeed in doing this the greater the gratitude will be that wells up in them for everything that, despite the situation, they have going for them. Small things can sparkle and become beautiful. An old woman put it this way: 'I can imagine that my new life can proceed from a small matter. For instance, if somebody feeds the birds every day, not too much. The weakest shall become the strongest.' This kind of slowing down and intensification of the speed of life radiates as gentle goodness out into the surroundings. Children are especially grateful if they may live in this kind of atmosphere.

# 4. The Bone Man

How does it happen that old people are by no means always as virtuous as they ought to be according to the previous chapters? There are old men who are greedy for power and who sometimes go so far as to lead the fate of nations to disaster. And are there not old women who dress up in a most embarrassing way to show off their vanity? Are not many old people ungrateful, grumbling, aggressive, domineering, miserly and dissatisfied?

The fruits of old age do not come to us as a gift. Bad qualities that we have not overcome in the course of our life appear in old age in an even worse form, often in that of a caricature. This also applies to the temperaments. Someone who was a bit melancholic in their younger years will, if it is not overcome at the proper time, become dissatisfied and constantly grumble. Anyone who was spoilt in life, and who therefore floated on the surface, will, if no deepening occurs, become childish in old age. Not only does the body become sclerotic, but soul qualities become rigid, too.

Growing old is a constant battle: a fight against tiredness and exhaustion, against weakness, clumsiness, forgetfulness, lameness, illness and loneliness, but also against clinging to possessions, against meanness, lack of trust, egoism and various kinds of fear. One has the experience of being squeezed out of one's bodily house, and one sets out to protect oneself against it and holds on to what one can.

Parallel to this there is also the problem of how life will manage to continue. It is difficult to find people who are ready to provide help. It is difficult to accept help, by putting oneself in someone else's hands. In earlier days it was obviously the family that gave the help as well as they could, and considered it right to do so. That it is not only love that is given is described here in the following little story passed on to us by the brothers Grimm.

## *The Old Grandfather and his Grandson*

There once was a man who was extremely old and whose eyes had grown dim, his ears deaf, and his knees shaky. When he sat at table these days he could hardly hold his spoon, and he splashed soup onto the tablecloth—some of it dribbled out of his mouth as well. This made his son and his son's wife so sick that at last they made him sit in the corner, where they gave him his meal in an earthenware bowl. This made it even harder for him to eat. As he looked longingly across at the table, with tears in his eyes, his hands shook so much that he dropped and broke his bowl. The young woman scolded him, but all he could do was sigh. She then bought him a wooden bowl, out of which he now had to eat. As they sat there like that the little grandson, who was four years old, got down from the table and began putting some sticks together. 'What are you doing?' asked his father. 'I am going to make a little trough,' answered the child, 'for you and mother to eat out of when I am grown up.' The man and the woman looked at one another for quite a while, and then they began to cry; they fetched the old man back to the table and from then on he always sat with them again, and they said nothing when he sometimes spilt something.

Stories like this, and much worse ones too, even happen today. Love for a helpless child can to a certain extent be taken for granted. But even this is becoming less and less a matter of course, still less the love for an old person.

Consequently many old people prefer today to take the step of going into a home for the elderly so as not to be a burden on their families. Or there is no family. In a home there is a neutral staff of carers, who are paid for their services. This also has its problems, too, of course. In the future a lot of imagination will probably have to be developed in this social field to enable there to be an individual approach possible in old age. In any case it is not easy to let go of one's pattern of life, to leave one's house, to part from many things one is attached to and to give up a part of one's independence. What forces us to do this is one's own body, which obeys one's will less and less. It is drawn under the spell of gravity. One has also to reckon with the occasional fall, because either one did not see the obstacle properly or one was too clumsy — or because one's brain failed to do its work for a moment. When one's legs finally don't want to carry one any more and one has to spend one's days sitting or lying, sores and abrasions easily arise. Now we notice for the first time how strongly the forces of gravity work in a body when its mobility has gone.

It becomes clearer and clearer that human beings are not identical with their bodies but that these are their instruments, which earlier on were more willing but now resist moving. This realization can lead one to acquire a relationship with one's body that is distanced in a friendly way. There are some old people who can take this with a lovely sense of humour. During an illness Rainer Maria Rilke wrote a poem about this:

> Brother body is a poor fellow . . . : This means, to
>     him, being rich.
> *He* was often the rich one: so we will forgive him
> the poverty of his bad moments.
> When he behaves as though he hardly knew us
>     any more
> we may gently remind him of all we have in
>     common.
> Of course we are not one person but two lonely
>     people:
> Our consciousness and him;

But how much do we have to thank each other
   for,
as friends do! And we find out when we fall ill:
Friends have a hard time of it!

The more distanced we are from 'brother body' the
more we can notice a foreign power pushing its way
into the body and nestling itself there in the bones: the
spirit of stiffness, the bone man.

Once, when I wanted to help my mother wash
herself, I said: 'Do you have to keep your hands so
tightly clenched? Open them, so that we can wash
them more easily!' 'That wasn't me, that was the bone
man,' was the answer, which gave me a lot to think
about. What do we go through when a foreign being
has nestled itself into our body, which ought to belong
to us?

We are disconcerted to see that in lonely rooms
old people who are ill are fighting an occult, a hidden battle against demonic beings that are not incar-
nated in flesh and blood yet can overpower our
body. Are these the 'lords of darkness', who are up
to their mischief in the darkness of this present age,
which Paul writes about in his letter to the Ephe-
sians (chapter 6:12). There is a heroism that doesn't
manifest itself in outer deeds but solely through
human existence. We begin to understand the scene
Rudolf Steiner tells us about when a lady on seeing
a very old person who lay lame in bed, and had to
be fed, said, with great sympathy, wouldn't it be a

good thing if this poor soul were released soon. To which Rudolf Steiner answered most seriously: 'By no means, every hour that she still lives on earth is important for the whole of humanity.' Confrontation with resistance in the bodily organization is a deed equal to anything else we can contribute to world progress.

The body cannot only become estranged; it can become a tormentor, as Rainer Maria Rilke speaks about in a rarely heard poem with the following message:

> Come thou, the last one I acknowledge,
> unholy pain in bodily tissue:
> The way I burnt in the spirit, see, I am
> burning in you; The wood has for a long time
> been reluctant to approve of the flame that you
> blaze with, but now I nourish you and burn in
>   you.
> My local mildness becomes in your fury a hellish
> fury that is not from here.
> Purely, without plan or future I ascended onto
> the stake of confusing pain
> assured of nowhere bringing anything for the
>   future
> for this heart, whose content was silent.
> Is it still I who burns unrecognizably?
> I am not pulling in any memories:
> O life, life; Being outside.
> And I in the blaze. Nobody who knows me.

To give the body up to burning with pain is the last gift we can give to mankind. It has a significance that is far above the personal level. It is a following, an imitating of Christ on the path of the Passion to spiritualizing physical substance, towards building up the resurrection body. To live in an old body that has become brittle or ill is a contribution to the overcoming of Ahriman, the Spirit of Darkness. Those people who are in a position to be able to care for the old and sick are also doing this.

# 5. The Swaying of the Walls

Death has many faces. And these go through change, both in the life of individual human beings and in human evolution as a whole. In ancient Greece the image of the violent god of death became milder. It acquired gentler features and became the brother of sleep.

With the coming of Christianity familiarity with death withdrew more into the life of the soul. People lived with it. St Francis of Assisi included it in his praise of creation:

> Praised be thou, O Lord, for bodily death, our
> brother,
> from whom no living creature can escape.
> Woe to those who die in mortal sin.
> Blessed are those who are in a state of grace,
> night will bring them no hurt.

If death is to be a friend and brother to human beings the battles and efforts in this regard must have been anticipated beforehand.

This was how it was with my mother whose death I am reporting. The transition happened almost unnoticed. The finality of the last breath, however, brought time to a standstill. It was as though a great winged being descended, filling everything with its peace.

The Greeks imagined that an initiate has a different relationship to death than a non-initiate. Initiates do not go to the dark realm of the shades. Hermes, who accompanies souls, leads them directly into the domain of the Blessed. They have anticipated in their initiation the journey through the underworld and the confrontation with the forces of death. It can still be the same today.

We can add to this that apart from the initiation that is acquired consciously along the path of training severe strokes of destiny or an advanced old age can bring an initiation in life, by means of which the after-death shocks are suffered in advance. May we assume that such people may ascend faster after death into the 'domain of the Blessed', in other words the spiritual world.

Elderly people approaching death can feel themselves experiencing something for which they lack any concepts of understanding. They can only speak about it in pictures, which, although these are taken from the sense world, make no sense realistically. These are confusing for their companions, like when a sick person is delirious. However, if those people who are accompanying the death can manage not to allow their 'normal mind' to be the judge of things but to open themselves to the pictures, they can learn a great deal and experience a huge inner deepening. They can also help the old person by trying to 'interpret' the pictures, and by doing this bring more consciousness into the process.

Old people often suffer a great deal from the lack of understanding in the carers. Then they try to hide their situation, and they say things like this: 'I would be able to hide it tonight, when they come, but I will not always be able to do that.' Or: 'You could say that it is an illusion, but I have to put up with it.' How upsetting this can be is seen in the following statements. 'I am between two worlds, and I have the feeling, now, that I can talk to you about it. But the other matter is also true. The sisters always insist that they are right. All I say is wrong and all they say is right. But if it stays like that I am going to go crazy.'

Another lady obviously did not have the same problems with those around her, though she did experience a similar relationship: 'I have seen a lot on my life's journey, and when the sun comes out it all goes again. That makes me think that it has all been a deception. But that is not true: it is supernatural. It is still here, so I know that it is not a deception.

'I have to be critical of it all the time, and ask time and again: is all that I experience really true? Ought we not, all of us, to be examining the world and learning how it runs according to its own laws?

'I travel on and on through one world after another, experiencing indescribable things — and then I find myself in my bed again, in familiar surroundings. That is absolutely shattering.'

In the booklet *A Way of Self-Knowledge* (GA 16)[*]

---

[*]SteinerBooks, Great Barrington 2006.

Rudolf Steiner describes pictorial experiences on the path of spiritual training which are characteristic of the first step into the elemental world:

> A moment can occur when the soul feels, inwardly, quite different from usual. Usually it will start by feeling as though one's soul were passing from sleep into an enlivening dream. Only we know from the beginning that this experience cannot be compared with what we otherwise know as dreaming. One is then totally removed from both the sense world and the thought world and yet one has the kind of experience one has in ordinary existence when one confronts the outer world in a waking state. One feels urged to visualize this experience. One brings to it the kind of concepts that one has in ordinary life, but one knows for certain that this is a different experience from that to which these concepts usually apply. We consider these merely to be means of expression for an experience we have not had before, and that we know would be impossible to have in ordinary existence. One feels kind of entirely surrounded by storm clouds. One hears thunder and sees lightning. Yet one knows one is in a room of a house. One feels infiltrated by a force that one knew nothing about before. One then imagines one sees cracks in the walls around one. One is prompted to say either to oneself or to someone one

imagines is beside one: now something tremendous is happening; lightning is striking through the house, and strikes me; I feel myself taken hold of by it. It dissolves me—When a series of such visualizations have taken place then one's inner experience returns to the normal one.

Pictures such as these that Rudolf Steiner describes are an expression of our release from the body, of our becoming alienated from the world of space, from the swaying of what we believe to be firmly fixed, the crumbling of the visible walls. It is like experiencing the ground being pulled away from under our feet. This is similar to what the dying often experience years before their actual death. So we can understand what our mother means when she says things like the following.

'There are no proper walls here. These are just pieces of cloth hanging there.'

'Where does it go down to from here? That looks like such a very narrow chicken run going up there. I will hardly be able to go up there.'

'I would just like to know what it will be like here when it is cold. The walls really are so thin, aren't they? Just like sheets.'

People experience the increasing brittleness of the body as an increasing thinning of the walls, as a losing of all our sheaths. 'They have simply pulled my vest off over my ears, and here I stand totally naked in the middle of the room where everyone can see in through the windows.' Many a person will have experienced something like this in a dream.

It contributes a lot to our security in life if we have a place where we feel at home, 'our own four walls' into which we gladly retreat. But now we begin to have doubts about these four walls. We want to get out, we long desperately to 'go home'. We get annoyed when the carers keep leading us back into this room, which we cannot accept any more. Somehow or another we sense that we have no longer got anywhere to stay, but have to be moving on, alone, in total uncertainty as to where we are going.

'I have to go all on my own. All you others are leaving me!'

'You cannot be of any help to me. I have to go the other way. Only I do not know which one it is.'

I am full of doubts and fears. 'I will surely hardly be able to get there if I am afraid of going on my own.'

'I keep thinking: whatever will I meet with, whatever will I meet with?'

But inexorably, implacably, I have to go on. 'During the last week I have lost so much. And I do not mean that outwardly, but inwardly.'

'Up till now all this has been child's play. But now it is going to get serious!'

# 6. The Body as a Prison

If I only knew what I can catch hold of firmly! The feeling of falling, of losing one's support, having no dwelling-place, no protective sheath round one is the aspect of existence one can experience when one's living structure is loosening and the feeling of security in sense existence is being exposed to the ocean of the etheric world. 'I let myself go! I let myself fall. There is no place to go, and I shall not be able to find one!'

One is leaving space, and one will soon be leaving time as well. Many old people can no longer distinguish between day and night. It is of help in this situation to have a firmly fixed daily routine.

A different sort of uneasiness arises from the fact that the physical body still has strong hold of one, has one in its clutches. Here, too, my old mother had to put up with a lot of depressing, dreamlike images. Sometimes, if she was asked, she told me what these dreams were.

'I was going for a walk, and I came down to the station I know and went in and found that it looked like my home at one moment and then at another moment it didn't. And I went inside, for I wasn't properly dressed, having no shoes or stockings on, and I went down to the cellar. And a church was there — or a town hall — and a lot of people were there who were all bossing me around. In the afternoon or the evening a kind of divine service was scheduled to be held, and I thought: no way can I take part in it. I told them they should let me go home, but they wouldn't let me out. I said: ''Leave me alone, I don't want to be imprisoned.'' But they said I was crazy — so I slept in the church that night.'

'Time and again there were hindrances in my way. Everything was untidy, very narrow, where I had to push my way through the iron railings and cardboard boxes.' And the anxious question arose: 'where I shall go now with my bare feet.' It reminded me of the Dream Song of Olaf Åsteson, where the traveller in the world beyond has to go barefoot over the heath of thorns. And his clothes are torn to shreds:

> First of all I was driven out of my senses
> as I went over the heath of thorns.
> My scarlet garment was torn
> and also the nails of both my feet.

At one time my mother lived constantly with the image of being in prison. Mihailo Mihailov wrote in prison: 'This sort of experience is important for everyone to have, not only for those who live in a condition of outer imprisonment but for everyone who has ever lived on earth or may still live on it. It is of the utmost importance to be absolutely clear on the matter that prison and concentration camps, i.e. the kind of arbitrariness that can under no circumstances restrain the forces of the visible world, await everyone sooner or later. Illnesses, catastrophes, accidents and death are no different from being arrested, put on trial, or put into prison or a concentration camp. Nobody can evade such things. Maybe those who have been spared the experience of a lack of freedom assume that there is a significant difference between life in prison and outside it, but those who have lived in captivity will begin instinctively to grasp the fact that the difference between them is quite superficial and temporary and that for everybody the free world will at some time become a death cell.'

Statements like the following are to be seen and understood against this background.

'I am so afraid that I have got to live in prison, for that is quite a different world.'

'We are caught! You will not get out any more, and without you neither can I.'

'The front door will surely be locked. If you ring it will certainly be the end. Then we shall be separated.'

'I have been wondering whether if I pay them they will let me go.'

'Why is it all closed off here?'

Or even:

'Don't you realize that the police have come for me?' This is an astonishing remark for a person who during her whole lifetime had no dealings with the police.

Such experiences must be connected with panic.

'I am so afraid. Who can possibly lift me out of this?'

'It is written in the shadows: Fear and anxiety! You probably cannot see it.'

The attachment to the physical body with all its limitations and infirmities includes being more and more dependent on help from other people. That alone is agonizing. For after all one is not a child who does not know any better. As far as one knows one has become an independent person. One would far prefer to do a lot of this for oneself. It is embarrassing to have other people do intimate things for one. One is also ashamed that one is in this condition. It is no wonder that help is often not accepted in a friendly and grateful manner, but that one resists it and is stubborn. That is not always easy for the carers. They are full of good will to do their best, and are ticked off for it. It could be of help to them if they were to imagine the inner situation of the old person really concretely. There is in the Gospel a scene where Jesus says to Peter: 'When you were young you dressed yourself and went where you wanted to go. But when you are old you will stretch out your hands and someone else will dress you and lead you where you do not want to go.'

'Where do you want to go?' I asked my mother, when she wanted to go out of the door.

'Where there is freedom,' was the answer.

# 7. Masks

Many an experience in the approach to death opens easily to the enquiring mind, although many of them are difficult to interpret. Many a deceptive world pushes its way in and mixes with ordinary day consciousness. Pictures emerge, masklike creatures created by our own soul, and need to be overcome in some way.

What were the many strange 'children' in my mother's sickroom meant to be? That was about the time she began to need full-time care in a situation she did not feel happy in, not comfortable with, not 'mothered'. Sometimes she volunteered information about these creatures, and sometimes she told us about them when we asked her to. To begin with she spoke about a kind of sculptured figure with a black or red cap on its head and a distorted face. A lot of them stood around on the shelves. 'Can't you see them?'

'No.'

'Then you have got bad sight!'

Later on she wondered where all the children came from. They were all naked, and they appeared to be 'not quite normal'. Sometimes she described them as black or brown. Their eyes were either shut or stuck down with sticking plaster. They also appeared to be dumb and seldom without an expressive face. But sometimes their faces were spotted or painted with a glaring colour, as the 'figures' before were. There were more and more of them, and their increasing numbers was frightening. Occasionally there were grown-up ones among them, too. But they all looked horrible. Only seldom did she describe concrete scenes, for instance: 'Over there they have all set something up for the children's afternoon rest. They look as though they are dead.'

Occasionally there were a few more appealing pictures: 'I say, what sort of little boy is that, that you have hanging on your arm?'

In answer to the question as to where all those creatures could have come from, in *her* opinion, *she* was attracting them!

After a change in the whole external situation, when a secure and familiar routine was set up, these creatures immediately disappeared without trace and never appeared again.

# 8. One with the Environment

What could be more beautiful than a morning in the solitude of a Greek landscape? It is spring. The song of blackbirds, tits, hedge sparrows and sometimes even a nightingale resounds through the air. Down in the small valley the stream gurgles. The plane trees are standing there in their first light green. Olive trees, rustling in a light breeze, march up the slope. Up here it is full of colourful flowers. Filled with warmth, surrounded by light, the life of human beings and nature intermingles. One is aware that soul life is no longer imprisoned in separate coverings but that feeling expands and spreads out over the whole valley right up to the ether blue of the sky.

We probably visualize that a soul is actually located in far too small and narrow a place. Don't we all interpenetrate one another? Do we not to a large extent live in soul within one another? Doesn't it often happen that one person says what the other person is just thinking about, especially in the case of people who are psychologically close to one another? But children and old people too, have a lot of sensitivity in this direction. It was quite remarkable to what extent my old mother identified herself with her surroundings, a sensitive indicator of every mood. And she did this, too, or did this especially at moments when she looked as though she was asleep.

This could happen to a curious extent. One morning it occurred to me that I ought to write an urgent postcard to Berlin. I did this, and then went to my mother's bedside, who received me with the words: 'I have to write to Berlin!' Then there was the occasion when she urgently wanted to have a hot compress, just when a member of the family was complaining about having toothache. And she felt under strain when someone was cleaning the windows in her room. 'I have had to clean the windows the whole morning! That is too much for me.'

No, an old person occupies more space than just a seat in an armchair. They fill the whole house. And like a sensitive musical instrument they register harmony and a loving attitude, but also any tension or disharmony in their surroundings. One mustn't imagine for a moment that when their consciousness dies down and their eyes are closed almost all the time that they are not perceiving anything. A wide-awake exclamation will suddenly prove that they were fully aware of what was going on. Of course, one could also say that it was more an inner perception than an outer one. The boundaries between the inner and the outer world become blurred. They identify themselves with the people who surround them. This is how we should understand the groan: 'When will the time come when I can finally lead my own life again?'

'What sort of a life do you lead, then?'

'Yours.'

So they don't only lose hold of both space and time, but they also lose hold of themselves and their own separate soul life.

This happens especially when there is a deep inner connection between the person who is being cared for and her carer. Rudolf Steiner speaks about this in a lecture given on 16 June 1923 (GA 30, lecture 6). It was a case of a daughter cared for by her mother.

> The daughter finds it very pleasant to have her mother looking after her. She feels her mother's love for her. In such a moment when one of them is so aware of the love coming from the other one, and, in addition, is very weak, the strange phenomenon occurs that this person no longer thinks with their own astral body. This becomes dull, and the astral body of the other person acquires the upper hand. Then it can even happen that one begins to think with the other person's thinking. So it has happened that while the mother was looking after the daughter this feeling conferred itself so strongly onto the daughter that the daughter began to feel and think just like her mother.

A heavy responsibility falls here on the person who is the stronger of the two and who in this case has the 'upper hand'. On the one hand the other person needs support not only bodily but also psychologically, but on the other hand however much love there is there ought to be as much freedom as possible — so that person must be able inwardly to hold herself in check.

Again, one must not assume that a person who is ill, old or handicapped is only weak. Despite how weak they are there is a lot of strength coming from them. Even the need for help cannot presuppose that the person living with them can automatically follow their own interests. When they go out they do not just leave the house, but leave a house that has a grandmother in it. That is what connects the family set-up. Perhaps neighbours, too, are included in this. Every community has its own particular kind of priority and intensity. The old person can be felt to be the soul of the house and become the social centre of the family. The family's life organism is held together by this communal task. The 'burden' of a person needing care, the demands made by her, are an important contribution to the maintenance of a human community.

In the case of an old person whom one has known earlier on there is certainly, running parallel to this, a painful experience that the person is slipping away more and more as a partner, and becoming less and less directly within reach. Life experiences that were not imparted up till now will not come your way any more. The condition may last a very short time or for a very long time. This is the time in which old friends eventually withdraw. For a period of time someone else may step in as a replacement, for instance a son who, sitting beside his own mother, had a conversation with one of his mother's friends who had come on a visit. The old mother just sat there apathetically not saying a word. Afterwards, when the friend had gone, she said in a wide-awake voice to her son: 'You stood in for me very well!'

Right until the end bodily care forms a strong bond between people. But this bond lies right down in the sphere of the unconscious. So then the question can arise: how can one still appeal directly to a person's soul when conversation isn't possible any more? What kind of messages can get through?

For a certain while one can give them pleasure by reading to them. But it is not at all easy to find the right reading matter. It must not be too intellectually demanding, but easy books chosen merely for entertainment can make them impatient. What a waste of time! What about biographies? This is possible for a while, but then it suddenly becomes clear that this sort of material is no longer suitable, either because the listener can no longer distinguish herself from what she hears or does not see how she relates to it.

Superficial subjects cannot penetrate any more. 'A lot of words spoken physically don't come through to me.' But what *did* come through to her were verses or rhythmic prose. The rhythm of language penetrates more deeply than anything conceptual. Cultic language, a cultic act acquires quite new significance now. One can experience what a real help communion for the sick can be. Out of three spheres of life, science, art and religion, religion is the force that accompanies human beings the longest on their life's path.

We begin reading a passage of the Bible each evening, which was obviously a welcome activity, and gave rise to the following remark: 'And many thanks for the lovely sermons that you have given me every evening.'

A remarkable thing was that she maintained her sense of humour right to the end. Amusing conversations in her presence were obviously perceived leading to unexpected humorous comments or a sudden laugh in response to a joke. It certainly did her good to be able to share such moments with an intimate family circle. Occasionally she observed: 'That was nice that I could have such a jolly time this evening, because I am often really depressed when I am in the throes of this devil!'

# 9. Soul Purification

I gaze into the darkness
Within it there arises light,
living light.
Who is this light in the darkness?
It is I myself in my reality.
This reality of the I
Does not enter into my earthly life,
I am but a picture of it.
But I shall find it again
When, with good will for the Spirit,
I shall have passed through the Gate of Death.

*Rudolf Steiner*

Indeed, she was obviously often aware of being in 'the throes of the devil', and this, too, was a cause of oppression and fear.

After death the soul sees itself confronted with its life's failings, a period that the old Christian faith called purgatory and Indian wisdom kamaloca. Before the soul has been purified and has passed through the cleansing fires it cannot be taken up into the pure life of the spiritual world. It passes once again, backwards, through its life. Its aberrations and weaknesses appear before it. It becomes painfully aware of how it has trespassed against other people, of what it could have done better. During earthly life it covered this up time and again. In the bright light of the spirit it suddenly stands out very clearly. The lawful nature of the world is moral; it is our fate to be judged accordingly.

When a person has lived a long life and has had one foot in the beyond for a long time many a thing can be anticipated during the life on earth that other people are confronted with after death. That it is actually oneself who is the devil that is doing the tormenting is also basically obvious.

To the question 'What are you actually afraid of?' the prompt answer was: 'Of myself!' Many of the things she said shows a strong, morally tinged experience that was not understandable out of direct daily life. Possibly comments like this came from this kind of feeling: 'I said something nasty, and for this I beg for your forgiveness.' But not fragmentary remarks that came out again and again quite abruptly:

'Sackcloth and ashes and everything we have to learn here...'

'Oh mother, mother! My failings are such and such.' This was said literally.

'Can you give me the address?'

'Whose address?'

'Of the person I have wronged. I really want to confess what I did wrong.'

'We have no reason to feel satisfied. For after all we have accumulated debts.'

Sometimes statements like this came first thing in the morning, as the first words after waking up:

'I have such a bad conscience.'

'I am so ashamed.'

'There is so much I should have done.'

'What do you say about the unhappiness I have instigated?'

Morality does not only express itself as consciousness of guilt but also as the will to help. For instance: 'We could help various people...' What followed was unfortunately not understandable. Some people experience this aspect in particular, this necessity to help especially intensively and consciously.

It was like this in the case of another old woman: 'We must help one another. Otherwise we cannot live.'

'Help one another! To help—that is the greatest thing we can do.'

The philosopher Schelling writes in his philosophical conversation 'Clara or about the Connection between Nature and the World of Spirits' that he wrote astonishingly and consistently directly after the death of his wife who he loved more than anyone else about this after-death, in-between state of soul purification:

> For only a few souls pass over so purely and free of all love for earthly matters that they can immediately be absolved and arrive at the highest place. But even those in whom no ill will

ever took root, but in whom the original seed of the Good often lay hidden under the thorns of the world and was impeded in its development, yet never damaged or quite destroyed, go over with so much vanity, wrong opinions and conceit and laden with other kinds of dishonest qualities that they stand no chance of straight away joining the company of the saints and the totally holy and healthy ones, but have first of all to go through a great deal of purification, some of them more and others less, according to what they are like, and have to spend on it. And such purification can certainly not proceed without great suffering.

These pains have to do with the exterminating of every illusion about our own excellence, the going through of every kind of doubt right through to the feeling of absolute nothingness. In a conversation with my mother about dying it was said that passing over into another condition of existence could also be a good thing. To which I received the prompt reply: 'Yes, if one does not extinguish oneself. Then one has to bear all that one has done wrong.'

Again and again it was possible to ascertain that in a condition that people like to call 'confused' the words that were spoken expressed the greatest truth and uncompromising conscientiousness. This was also seen in the fact that something that had been said was sometimes corrected. This is why we can take other statements fully seriously that showed that she had overcome something.

'Love, love, love—I am getting happier and happier!' And then, thoughtfully: 'After all, quite a number of things have already been revealed to me.'

# 10.  Returning to Childhood

When the Bushmen in inner Africa sense that their death is approaching they return to the place of their birth. They sometimes have to walk hundreds of miles to get there. For they are convinced that they can only be released from life in the place where they came into it.

Every old person, even in our civilization, can probably understand this need. But in actual fact it is usually not possible to put it into practice. So they carry out the journey inwardly and return to their childhood.

This can take the form that grandfathers or grand-mothers can speak for hours about the years of their childhood. They suddenly remember details that they had forgotten a long time ago. A different kind of memory arises here than the ordinary one that people from middle age onwards complain of losing.

A loss of memory can also occur on the path of spiritual training for higher knowledge. Rudolf Steiner does not think that this is anything to worry about. He suggests developing a new, pictorial memory instead. This certainly has quite a different quality than the abstract, intellectual memory that we work with in our schools.

The long-lasting memory of old people is also pictorial. The childhood memories simply arise unbidden. They can, finally, be so intense that old people enter into them completely and feel like children again. A person who was dying talked about playing in a sandpit. They call for their mothers, their siblings or childhood friends. Often, towards the end of their lives, they prefer to lie in a peculiar rolled up position, like an infant, almost like an embryo. A daughter was very shaken one troublesome day when then the only words she could understand her mother saying were: 'I want you to take me in your arms!'

But it is not only the content of the pictures in which an old person lives that points to this return to childhood, but also the fact that the old person expresses things entirely pictorially and not abstractly. This has its parallel in the years of childhood at the age when children tend to want to hear the wisdom of the world in the form of fairy tales.

Elisabeth Kübler-Ross, the well-known researcher on dying, turns our attention to the symbolic language of people who are dying. She had the experience that many of the people who are dying always want to talk about their death, even about the timing of it — not in actual plain words but hidden in pictures, so they are not always understood.

For instance they tell us about an old man who wanted to give her his stick. To begin with she didn't take this seriously. Not until she found him dead soon afterwards did it become clear to her what he was trying to express with his offer. For without his stick he couldn't walk at all. In wanting to give it away it meant that he no longer needed it. She regretted afterwards that she had not had the presence of mind to listen out for what he was intending to say, and had said: 'You don't need your stick any more then, do you?' He would have denied this, and they could have talked about what concerned him.

Old people are usually clearly aware whether death is already imminent or still a long way away. This became clear when her mother read her a passage from a book by Elisabeth Kübler-Ross. And she added: 'That is all so remote from me. Surely I still have a long way ahead of me.' That was four and a half years before her death. A little while later she said something similar: 'Thank you very much for all the trouble you take with me. I believe it will still last for a long time.'

Elisabeth Kübler-Ross has a number of examples in which departing from the earthly world is presented in a picture of a journey in a train. A patient told her: 'You will not believe what happened to me last night. I went through a big struggle. A large train was driving at great speed down a hill, and I was having a big fight with the train driver. I wanted him to stop the train a few millimetres sooner! Do you understand what I am saying?'

A year before her death her mother had a feverish bronchitis, and she was really bad. Nevertheless she thought that she had missed the train.

'They are really angry with me!'

'Who are they?'

'All of them.'

A few days later she established the fact that she would travel to the next stop. But she did feel that she had become considerably weaker after this illness, and complained that all she wanted was to go off on her travels. Later on, when they were saying that despite everything things were going really well for us, she said: 'Yes. But I can't remain in the train.'

Existence gradually became more and more agonizing: 'I cannot go on sitting here all the time waiting until the lady dies.' It is clear here that consciousness can, and at one and the same time be on two levels. The result was the sad confirmation: 'I was not collected.' In response to the remark 'You were ordered and then not collected?' she had to laugh. It still went on for seven months until she was really 'collected'.

If we think about this return of an old person to childhood we come more and more to the idea of circles of time. The lines of life do not go straight ahead but are circular or, better still, rising spirals. The circles of life push their way into one another. One grows from one to another. It is the same with the human circles we grow through. A little child needs the older generation to care for it and guide it—its weal and woe depends on it. Then our school friends follow, student friends, career colleagues, the people one is connected with because one is in the same field at work. Then each change of place brings a new circle of friends. And the older one becomes the more contact one has with younger people, one's own children and their friends, with pupils and students who want to learn from one, but from whom one can and must learn a lot if one does not want to remain behind the times. We have to experience some, or even many, of the friends of one's own age passing over the threshold of death before one does oneself.

Then at the end, as in one's first childhood, a relationship of depending on other people can arise through the necessity of needing to be cared for. Through this there arises once more an absolutely new circle of human beings consisting of helpers, nurses and doctors, all of whom are younger than the patient. One is looked after by one's children and grandchildren, or those who could be such. And thus the ring of life is rounded off.

'There was once a grandmother with a granddaughter. When this little granddaughter was small she slept almost all the time and her grandmother baked the bread and swept the hut clean. She washed, sewed and wove for her grandchild.

'Many years later when the grandmother had grown old, she could not work any more, but lay close to the stove and slept a great deal. And then her grandchild baked the bread did the washing and the sewing and spun and wove for her grandmother.'

So Tolstoy tells us.

Doesn't a little story like this, which we were

repeatedly told in childhood, help give content and warmth to the relationship between a granddaughter and grandmother, and further between the young and the old?

# 11. Angel's Hands

In a letter to a very old friend Rudolf Steiner wrote to say:

> And now angel's hands are helping gradually to release you from the materiality and hardness of the body.
>
> This hurts, hurts very much, and you certainly often have more of a feeling of it being a punishment than a help, and yet this is the last thing that happens. What you are now suffering in the way of pain and which can transform into patience gives you the energy for a state of existence that you will be most grateful to receive.
>
> May you succeed in seeing through the clouds that sometimes want to spread pain in front of your inner eye and look through them to the kind but solemn countenance of the shaper of divine destiny who holds your destiny, your life and your suffering in his loving hands, and carefully lays upon you only as much pain as you can bear. He also gives you the strength never to be confused by it.

Each time a human soul leaves the earth it does so accompanied by and under the protection of its heavenly keeper, its guardian angel. As long as the person is in full possession of her earthly ego consciousness this being holds back. The person then carries the responsibility herself for her own actions. In childhood, before she has anchored herself firmly in her bodily sheaths, or in old age, when she is releasing herself from these again, she is in need of protection. This is why she lives in direct connection with the spiritual world, in the shadow of angel's wings, just the same way as it is at night in sleep.

> O Michael, who art above the angels
> and the just ones of Heaven,
> protect my soul
> with the shadow of thy wings,
> protect my soul
> on earth as also in the Heavens;
>
> From all the enemies on this earth,
> from all the enemies below this earth,
> from all the hidden enemies.
> Surround me and protect my soul
> with your wings,
> protect my soul with the shadow of your wings!

This ancient Irish prayer shows how people in earlier times prayed for the help of these angel beings. One can still do so today, for oneself or for someone else for whose welfare one feels responsible. One can ask the angel if one may be permitted to help this person. For the angels need the cooperation of people living on earth. When a human being can no longer control and care for her body then someone else must do it for her. A number of people can help do this, but there must be one particular person to whom the patient has given her trust and on whom she can depend and lean on both outwardly and inwardly. In the realm of pedagogy we use the somewhat cool expression *Bezugsperson*, or sponsor. One could call it a kind of godparent service. A godparent is a guardian or protector but the kind that does it not out of a material necessity like his parents do, but out of free will.

The good thing about it is that this act of protection is a mutual force. There are times in which one can oneself give protection, and other times when one is in need of protection oneself. It is even the case that whilst one is protecting someone else, on a different, higher level one is being protected by them. We are interwoven, go part of the way together.

Old people often have the feeling that things are like this, and often say so: 'I am so glad that you are accompanying me.'

'Where are you actually going, then?'

'Nowhere, other than above us. I am not in your way, and you mustn't think that I am.'

'In one way I am stronger than you, and in another way weaker. And you are stronger than I am and then you're weaker — like a protective service. We must not allow ourselves to be separated.'

Such a relationship cannot suddenly come to an end at death. For the time being when death occurs the body needs one more act of being cared for. It will be looked after and cared for one more time. We cover it with flowers like a spring meadow. Then it vanishes from view and the search for one's dear one cannot settle on any point in the sense world.

There are memories. These can be called up. They give us something to hang on to in the uncertainty, point in a certain direction. It is a good thing to remember scenes one has experienced with the deceased one, right as far as the kind of hand movements and the sound of their voice. But one also notices in the course of these efforts that one can come to the end of one's memories, and that there is a danger of becoming fixed on certain images. This is even more strongly the case if one possesses photographs on which the memory becomes fixated. Perhaps one is personally especially fond of one particular photo. But is it the one that is most characteristic of the deceased one? Which of the different pictures still applies after death. At what age was the person most 'herself'?

Looking for a relationship through gestures goes nowhere to start with. The deceased one is not here, the body is no longer responsive, and the soul is everywhere. Where is everywhere?

Whilst we are still in search of outer ideas there arises suddenly perhaps from within a picture that one feels is suitable. Is it true that the deceased are among us? Perhaps a deceased person appears to us as a delicate figure of light that illumines everything that happens and of which we know that it has accompanied all this with interest. We experience these happenings as being under its protection.

If we now look for another deceased person by means of a similar picture it is possible that one doesn't find her. One extinguishes this picture and gropes further. Suddenly a kind of rosebud appears in a reddish glow, and it is as though the deceased person said: 'You may imagine me like this. I am no enormous form of light. I really am still small. I still have to grow into the new world. The blossom that you see me still surrounded by are the hands of angels. And everything that you send me in the way of loving thoughts strengthens their power of protection. That is what you can do for me.'

To send thoughts into the spiritual world to a loved one who has died — one can perhaps find support for this in a verse, a prayer:

> May the love of my soul strive towards thee,
> may the love of my mind stream towards thee.
> May they sustain thee,
> may they enfold thee
> in spheres of love.
>
> *Rudolf Steiner*

We can live for quite a long time in such a picture, in a striving to do this. This does not mean that we have to do this all the time. One has to give the picture the chance to change. The bud will, of course, grow, and will unfold. Things go through a metamorphosis in the spiritual world, too.

So every death of a dear one is a call, a summons to the people left behind to add a new dimension to their thinking and actions, to cast off earthly limitations and to endeavour to go into the spiritual world with an ever-growing sensitivity and seriousness. Then we shall be capable of experiencing more and more what a dying woman felt like when she said: 'What a wonderful thing it is to come to God, even when it hurts!'

# 12. In Light-filled Heights

Hiking in Greece leads again and again to remains of past cultures. Between meadows full of glowing red poppies there lie ruins admired by tourists and maintained for their benefit. Even in isolated regions the beauty of nature is filled with the breath of the past. How this land did blossom when the many terraces on the side of mountains were still planted and cultivated! Haven't I even read that in olden times there were forests on these arid hills in which the mighty heroes of antiquity hunted wild animals? And where the landscape is now disfigured by a gigantic industrial complex didn't there once lie, embedded between cornfields, the place where the holy mystery of Eleusis was? Demeter, the great Goddess, is said to have had her place here, when she was grieving the loss of her beloved daughter, the virgin Persephone. Persephone, whose myth gives us the image of the human soul, was abducted by Hades, the god of the underworld. Death became wedded to the soul. Not until this moment, as characterized in this image, did human beings become entirely earthly, i.e. fully infiltrated by death forces.

Demeter, her mother, however, when she had to suffer this, sat sorrowfully on a stone in front of the palace of the king of Eleusis. In the course of her sadness she let her form wither away, and disguised herself so that nobody recognized her. 'She looked like an old woman who could no longer mother children and no longer receive the gifts of the goddess of love.' (Kerényi: *Mythology of the Greeks*.) So she sat at the side of the road, when the daughter of the king of Eleusis, fetching water, found her and reverently invited her into the palace. There she took over the task of nursing the late born son of the king, Demophoon. Under her care the child grew and flourished like a god, without food. Demeter held it every night in the fire, like a log of wood, to give it immortality, until the queen noticed this, and was horrified. Then the goddess left the palace in anger.

These images are telling us that at the same time as death entered human nature the seed of immortality was put into it. What externally appears to be destruction, being brought to the glowing point by fire, can, looked at imaginatively, mean the beginning of a new spiritual life. It is assumed that the Greeks, who were privileged to participate in the festival of the Eleusinian Mysteries, rose to the heights of seeing boys arising out of the fire. This brought them to understand, in a pictorial way, how birth and death are interlinked.

A particularly subtle point of this mythical narrative is the statement that Demeter, after the theft of Persephone, was not the same as before. Up till now she had had a flourishing form, but she now appeared in the image of an old woman. She, the goddess of fertility, took upon herself the forces of old age, and filled it with her being; that, however, means that she made it fruitful. From now on her strength shines into our human decaying forces, whilst the upbuilding half of life comes under the mastery of Eros, the god of love. Rudolf Steiner describes this change in the human constitution in times long passed in a series of lectures on Greek mythology (19 August 1911, GA 129):

> When Eros withdraws from human beings as they age then Demeter begins once again to have an influence on the human bodily organization. Then, in a certain respect, Demeter can get into the human bodily organization again, and then what is representative of fruitful chastity, compared to the Eros organization, steps into the foreground. And our attention is drawn to a deep mystery, a very powerful mystery, in the development of human beings, when we look in this way at the ageing of a human being—the transformation of the Eros forces into the Demeter forces.

It is up to us to track down whether in the process of growing old we really can't actually sense a very special quality: fruitfulness in the sense of creativity that does not have its origin in surplus vitality, 'fruitful chastity' or 'chaste fruitfulness' as the gift of the great goddess to modern humanity.

This is the direction in which the thoughts that were passing through my soul were moving as I stood in front of the ruins of the old Eleusinian place of worship, the place that used to awaken the greatest feelings of veneration and holiness in people. Looking at it produced helpless grief. All round it were factory buildings, cars, refuse—our civilization in its whole ugliness and destructiveness. In between were the disintegrated walls of the sanctuary, surrounded by a fence. In the middle of the fenced area was a rocky mound in which yawned the opening of a cave called the 'gate of Hades'.

The hill is not very high, though when one climbs it one has quite a panoramic view. And now, if one lets one's eyes gaze into the distance, one gradually sees more clearly the special quality of structure of the landscape. The hill rises up out of a wide plain, which at the back is surrounded and closed off by a circle of softly rounded mountains. Earlier on it was said to have been covered with cornfields. In front, the mountain top descends to the sea. But the mirror of the sea does not reach into an immeasurable distance; it forms a semicircle the boundary of which is the elongated island of Salamis. One can imagine that in earlier times when the structure of this terrain could be seen more clearly, the large, round enclosed plain, half water and half land, could have at one and the same time a feeling of being expansive and enclosed.

Coming back to the starting point we tried once more to decipher the area of the ruins. The longer we stood and looked at it the greater became our puzzled dejection. Finally our gaze rose from the piles of ruins to the tops of a few trees covered with the green of spring, with the wind playing in them, and then looked further up to the light-filled dome of heaven.

The impression this made is hard to describe. It was as though, up there, like being born out of the living, weaving Greek light, the summer-like goddess was hovering over her cornfields. Suddenly peace and joyousness filled one's soul and the certainty arose: what has reality in the spirit world is indestructible. Anything that does not find a body on earth any more because it has been damaged and destroyed arises to a higher form of existence there. Such a thing is always available, and is findable for someone who looks for it with their heart.

Doesn't this certainty belong to what Eleusis told us in the past, and tells us today? Perhaps the journey to this special geographical spot was necessary to enable us to arrive at this insight.

> O, may my soul linger
> In light-filled heights
> Where, in the sun's gleams,
> Friendly dragonflies, fluttering in the warm rays,
> Become wedded to living space;
> In thinking of me
> They weave out of the force of grief;
> I feel how they feel me,
> How they stream through me bringing warmth;
> In cosmic weaving the spirit melts
> Earth gravity to become future light.
>
> *Rudolf Steiner*

# Epilogue

This little book gives a memory picture of the last earthly days of my beloved mother who passed over the threshold of death on 8 March 1990 almost 90 years of age. During her long lifetime she gave a lot of love to her children and grandchildren who, when they were with her, always received the warmest participation in everything that moved them, as also did many other people around her. The depth of her sympathy admittedly arose out of a basically melancholic temperament that was sometimes overcome and that appeared more strongly at other times. A low point in this respect came in the Second World War with its painful experiences, especially in the summer of 1940 over the loss of her beloved life partner. Through this her life acquired a strong inclination to turn inwards. The question of life after death became a burning one for her. Through this she found the approach to the Christian Community and to anthroposophy, the world-view of which she made thoroughly her own in the following 40 years — a path along which she also took her own children.

In total contrast to her husband who, 50 years before her, was torn so abruptly from life, she had to pass through a long, laborious path to death. In 1979 she decided to move to an old people's home as her sight had deteriorated so much that she could no longer read. By doing this she had people around her who could read to her, and she could take part in a great many events. In 1985 it became necessary for her to move to the care department.

In the following year, whilst spending a remarkably harmonious and joyful Christmas with us, the 'family counsel', consisting of a daughter, a son-in-law and four grandchildren, decided to keep her at home and to try to look after her here — which actually happened for more than four years, that is, until her death.

It is, of course, a risk to take on such an obligation and responsibilities when there are other regular daily tasks to do. We were constantly in doubt. We kept on asking ourselves whether we could go on doing it. It was of course a task that could not be undertaken by one person only. Help was needed, increasingly every year. So we suffered the whole time from uncertainty. The fact was that help was always forthcoming when really necessary. We couldn't have planned it like that, but 'chance' made it happen that in the whole of the four years at least one of the grandchildren was always living at home. In addition to this there was always the indispensable help of the nurses from the Home Care Institute and one or two students. Nobody's holiday had to be missed because of grandmother. There arose more and more the confidence that help would be there when needed.

What counted as help was not only practical assistance but also every positive thought. And conversely, the statement that we really could not deal with such a major case of nursing at home was for a long time very discouraging. Encouragement and interest were experienced as real forces. Looking back I am filled with deep gratitude for everything that was given us in this direction.

It was also an important experience for me to discover that the anthroposophical *Study of Man* (GA 293)[*] was not only able to give fruitful impulses for the teaching of young people but also for growing old and dying. Otherwise the kind of activity described here would have been a purely charitable one. So alongside the activity of caring there arose at the same time an understanding that deepened our knowledge.

The thoughts in the second chapter on the metamorphosis of spirit onto the physical level and the physical onto the spiritual level in the course of life are based on the seventh lecture of Rudolf Steiner's volume of lectures 'The Bridge Between Cosmic Spirituality and Man's Physical Nature' (GA 202)[†] and those of the last chapter on the second lecture of the cycle *Wonders of the World, Ordeals of the Soul, Revelations of the Spirit* (GA 129)[‡]. In the period after death had occurred the three lectures of 22–24

---

[*] Rudolf Steiner, *Study of Man*, Rudolf Steiner Press, Sussex 2004.
[†] See *Universal Spirituality and Human Physicality*, Rudolf Steiner Press, Sussex 2014.
[‡] Rudolf Steiner Press, London 1963.

November 1915 were especially helpful (in 'The Spiritual Background of the First World War' (GA 174b)[*]. It speaks there very concretely about what we can do for the so-called dead, what they mean to us and how the physical and the spiritual world are interwoven.

Occupying ourselves with these thoughts we can become more and more concretely aware of the fact of how what we give to a dying person in the way of strength and love streams back to us after their death in abundance, for which we can only be deeply grateful. The experiences and thoughts I have described in this book are meant as an expression of this gratitude, in the hope that they will also mean something to other people who are in a similar position.

Almut Bockemühl
Dornach 1990

---

[*]Not translated.